Get ~~School~~

M~~ng~~

and ~~ng~~

Meet Bip, Bop, and Boo!

Bip the Cat knows all about number problems.

Bip supports your child's numeracy and science learning.

Cuddly Bop the Elephant likes words and stories.

Bop helps your child's language development.

Boo the Monkey loves make-believe play and art.

Boo encourages your child's creative, physical, and social skills.

How to use this book

- Use this book together. Read the activities aloud to your child.
- Help your child take off the stickers and put them the right way up into the space.
- Always stop before your child becomes tired. Return to the page the next time.
- Give plenty of praise and encouragement as your child completes each activity.
- Look for any opportunities for asking questions about grouping and matching objects in your child's everyday experiences. Page 30 gives some examples.

Senior Editor Deborah Lock
Designer Nicola Price
Illustrator Reg Silva
Pre-production Editor
Andy Hilliard
Art Director Helen Senior
Educational Consultant
Penny Coltman

First published in Great Britain by
Dorling Kindersley Limited
80 Strand, London, WC2R 0RL
Copyright © 2015 Dorling
Kindersley Limited
A Penguin Random House
Company
10 9 8 7 6 5 4 3 2 1
001—271138—July/2015
All rights reserved.

Without limiting the rights under
copyright reserved above, no part
of this publication may be
reproduced, stored in or

introduced into a retrieval system,
or transmitted, in any form,
or by any means (electronic,
mechanical, photocopying,
recording, or otherwise), without
the prior written permission of the
copyright owner.

A CIP catalogue record for
this book is available from
the British Library.
ISBN: 978-0-2411-8457-8

Printed and bound in China

The publisher wishes to thank
Atsuko Burnett for making Bip,
Bop, and Boo; Dawn Sirett for
editorial work. The publisher
would like to thank the following
for their kind permission to
reproduce their photographs:
(Key: a-above; b-below/bottom;
c-centre; f-far; l-left; r-right; t-top)

4 Fotolia: Eric Isselee (cra). **10 Fotolia:**
Jan Will (clb). **11 Fotolia:** Eric Isselee
(cra); Valeriy Kalyuzhnyy / StarJumper
(cl). **19 Dorling Kindersley:** Natural
History Museum, London (fclb, clb, crb,
fcrb). **26 Corbis:** Radius Images (cla,
cra, ca). **27 Corbis:** 68 / Ocean (cra,
fclb); Studio Ton Kinsbergen /
Beateworks (ca). *Stickers:* **Dorling
Kindersley:** Lister Wilder (tractor).
Fotolia: Anatolii (piglet); Melissa
Schalke (calf). **Photolibrary:** Digital
Vision / Martin Harvey (tiger).

All other images
© Dorling Kindersley
For further information see:
www.dkimages.com

A WORLD OF IDEAS:
SEE ALL THERE IS TO KNOW

www.dk.com

Contents

Animal families   4 - 5

Toy shelves   6 - 7

Ladybird twins   8 - 9

Animal patterns   10 - 11

Animal homes   12 - 13

Busy vehicles   14 - 15

Treasure island   16 - 17

In the garden   18 - 19

Inside or outside   20 - 21

In the playroom   22 - 23

In the wardrobe   24 - 25

Pretty flowers   26 - 27

Seaside fun   28 - 29

More activities to try!   30

Certificate   31

Animal families

Find the baby animal stickers.
Match them to their shapes.

Now **draw along*** the
dotted lines to help each
baby animal find its mum.

*Younger children can follow the
dotted lines with their fingers.

4

Bop says, "Point to each animal and tell me the noise it makes."

Toy shelves

Boo says, "Point to the toys that may make some noise."

Toy musical instruments

Find the missing toy for each shelf.
Match the toy stickers to their shapes.
Talk about the toys on each shelf.
Why is the drum on the red shelf?

Cuddly toys

Toy vehicles

Ladybird twins

Look at all the ladybirds.
How many spots does each
ladybird have?

Match each twin ladybird sticker to sit below the ladybird with the same number of spots.

Bip says, "Which ladybird twins have the most spots?"

Animal patterns

Look at the animals in these two groups.
What patterns on them can you see?

Stripy animals

Find a sticker of another
stripy animal.

Find a sticker of another animal with spotty patches.

Spotty animals

Boo says, "Look at pictures of other animals. Do they have spots or stripes or neither?"

Animal homes

Find the animal home stickers.
Match them to their shapes.

Bop says, "Name two animals that live in water."

Find a home for each animal.
Draw along* the dotted lines to match the animals to their homes.

*Younger children can follow the dotted lines with their fingers.

Busy vehicles

Beep! Honk! Vroom!
What do all these vehicles have?

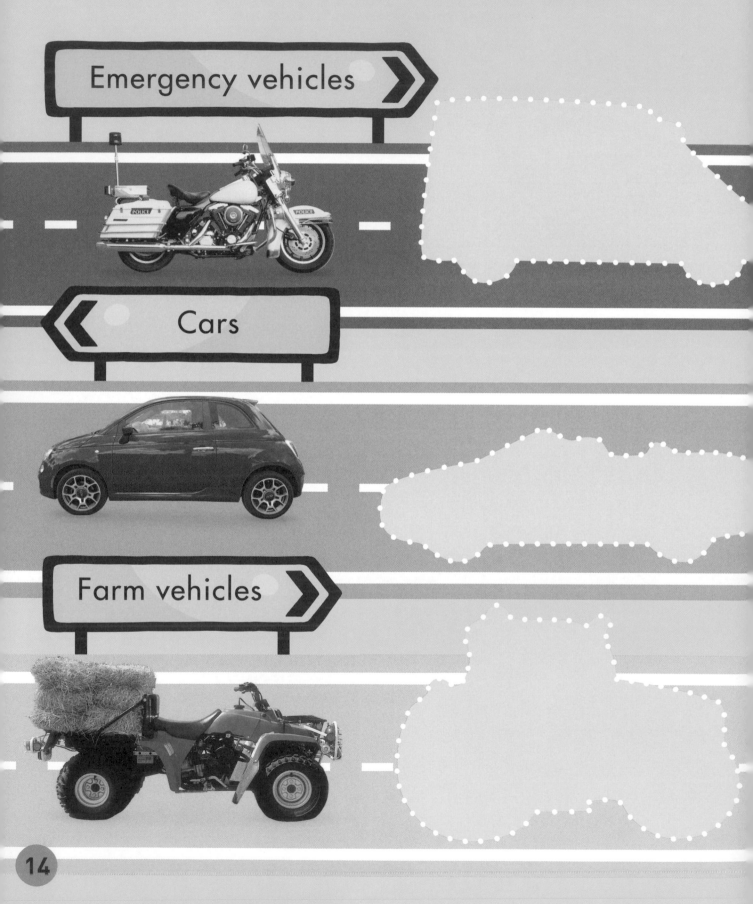

Emergency vehicles

Cars

Farm vehicles

Find the missing vehicle stickers
that belong on each road.
Talk about the vehicles along each road.

Boo says,
"Let's make the
noise of the fire
engine."

Treasure island

Follow the arrows to show
the way from the ship to the treasure.
Add the missing arrow stickers.

Key:

← left

→ right

↓ down

↑ up

Bop says, "Can you tell me how you get from your bedroom to your kitchen?"

In the garden

The garden needs tidying.

Find the things that are upside down, then **draw a circle*** around each one. The first circles have been drawn to help you.

*Younger children can point to the things that are upside down.

19

Inside or outside

Point to the things inside
the house and name them.

What can you see outside?

Boo says, "What games do you like to play outside? What do you play with inside?"

Find the missing stickers.
Put the stickers in the right place: in the house or outside.

21

Look at these things.
Some are short and some are long.

Find the sticker for
the long line of books.

Find the sticker to make the short
string of beads longer.

Point to the long pencils.
Point to the short pencils.

Bip says, "How many carriages does the long train have?"

Find 1 more train carriage to make the train even longer.

In the wardrobe

Find the odd one out in each row.
Draw a circle* around it.
The first circle has been drawn to help you.

*Younger children can point to the odd one out.

Pretty flowers

Draw along the dotted lines to match each flower to the vase of the same colour.

*Younger children can follow the dotted lines with their fingers.

Bop says, "Find some pictures of flowers. Sort them into groups of the same colour."

Seaside fun

Look at each row.
Each row makes a pattern.

What comes next?
Find the right sticker and
put it in the yellow box.

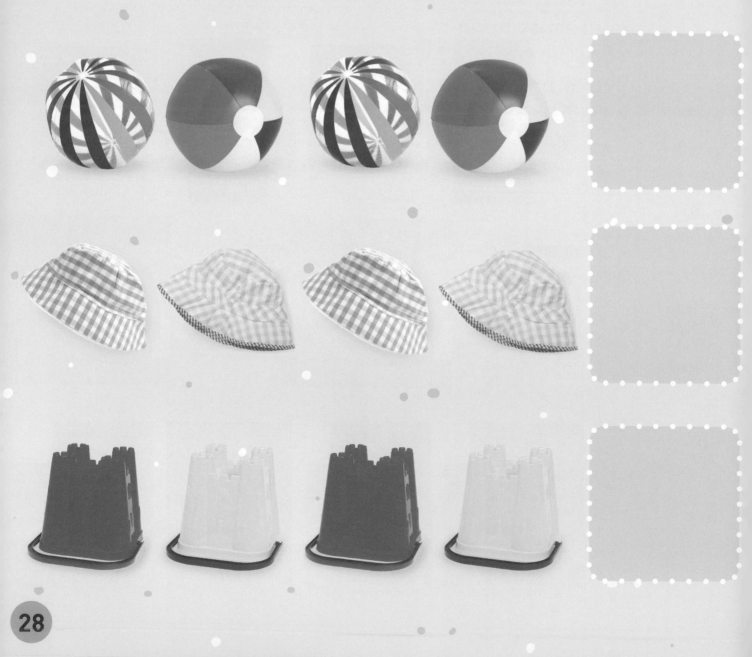

Boo says, "Make your own pattern with the starfish and fish stickers."

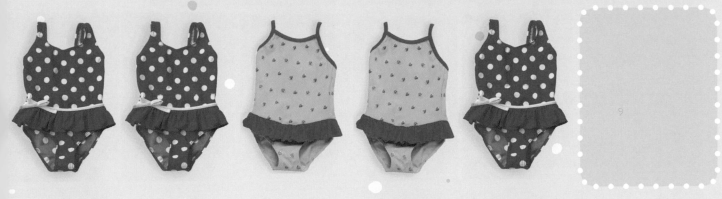

29

Put away forks and spoons in a divided drawer. **Match** the different types of cutlery in the different sections.

Sort a collection of buttons into groups of matching colours, or similar sizes or the same number of holes in them.

Sort a handful of mixed dried beans into matching shapes or a pile of dry autumn leaves into the type of tree. Hold one up and find 'another one like it'.

Help to sort and put away clean clothes. **Match** socks together as pairs. **Look** carefully at their colours and patterns.

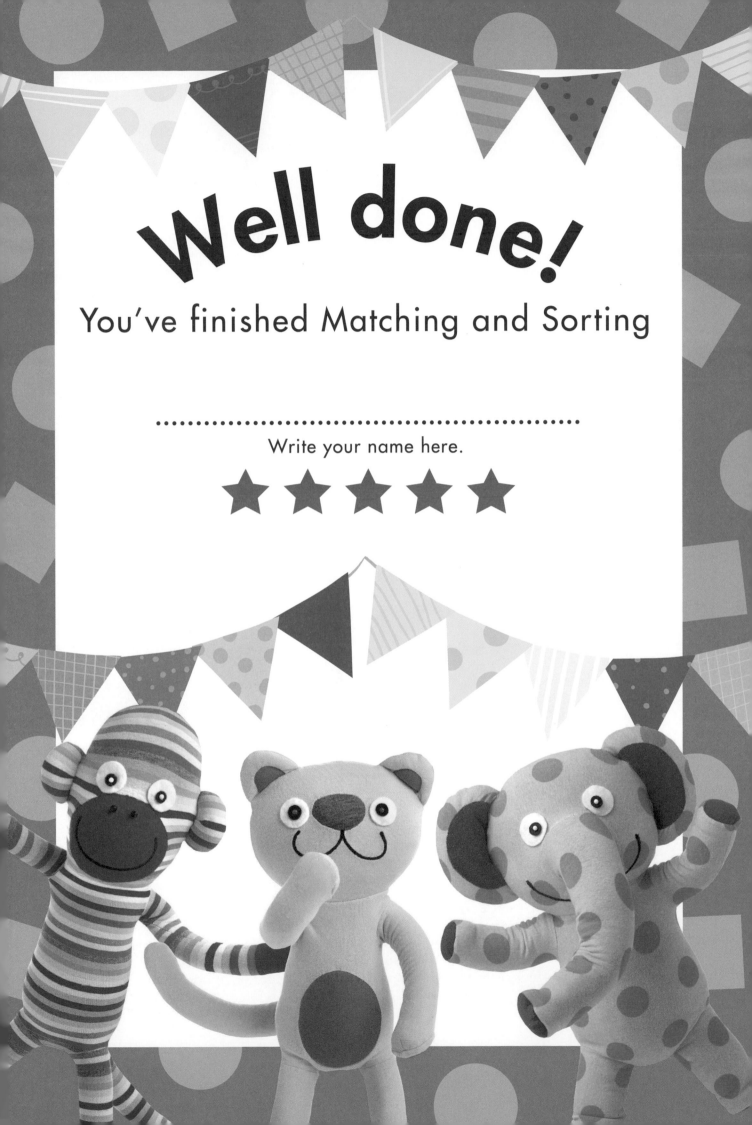

Well done!

You've finished Matching and Sorting

· ·

Write your name here.

★ ★ ★ ★ ★

From our Educational Consultant

DK always aims to offer content that prepares children for success in school and in life. In the DK **Get Ready for School** series, content is designed to address every aspect of a child's development, promoting important school-readiness skills such as critical thinking, creativity and communication.

The early years of a child's development really matter. As parents and carers we must take every opportunity to encourage our children and inspire their enthusiasm for learning.

This series offers the opportunity for children to learn through familiar topics, discussion and playful activities. Children reach stages at different ages, so this series builds on past progress and guides children onto the next steps.

I am happy to partner DK as consultant on **Get Ready for School**. Life is a learning adventure, and you are your child's best teacher.

Penny Coltman,
Early Years Educational Consultant

. . . .

The three levels of the **Get Ready for School** Playbooks reinforce and support your child's development. Children reach developmental milestones at different rates but follow a similar progression of stages. The activities in the playbooks follow these learning stages to develop your child's confidence, curiosity and independence.

Red Level 1 is for children who are beginning to make marks using a pencil, colouring and drawing; starting to recognise letters and numbers; beginning to develop the skills of counting and sorting; and showing interest in toys and the world around them.

Yellow Level 2 is for children who are handling a pencil and scissors with increasing control; beginning to notice and recognise familiar words around them; matching numbers and quantity, and comparing objects; and using their experiences to imagine, construct, explore and question.

Green Level 3 is for children who are bursting with growth in reading, writing, speaking and listening; looking closely at similarities, differences, patterns and change; beginning to apply adding and subtracting to solving problems; and constructing, imagining and experimenting with a purpose.

Pages 4 - 5

Pages 6 - 7

Pages 8 - 9

Pages 10 - 11

Pages 12 - 13

Page 20

Page 21

Pages 16 - 17

Reward stickers

These stickers are just for fun!